First published in 2017
by Jessica Kingsley Publishers
73 Collier Street
London N1 9BE, UK
and
400 Market Street, Suite 400
Philadelphia, PA 19106, USA

www.jkp.com

Copyright © Lisa Gutwein 2017
Illustrations copyright © Rowan Ambrose 2017

Front cover image source: Rowan Ambrose.

Library of Congress Cataloging in Publication Data
A CIP catalog record for this book is available from the Library of Congress

British Library Cataloguing in Publication Data
A CIP catalogue record for this book is available from the British Library

ISBN 978 1 78592 357 9
eISBN 978 1 78450 696 4

Printed and bound in China

Doorkins the Cathedral Cat

Lisa Gutwein

Illustrated by Rowan Ambrose

Jessica Kingsley Publishers
London and Philadelphia

Dedicated to the Cathedral Vergers;
custodians of the cathedral, custodians of the cat.

Thank you to the Southwark Cathedral staff,
congregation and wider community for sharing
their photographs and stories of Doorkins.

In the middle of London, between the office blocks and market stalls, stands the magnificent grand cathedral.

And in the cathedral lives a very special cat, named Doorkins.

Doorkins feels very lucky to have such a remarkable home. The very best thing about living in the cathedral is all the different people she gets to meet.

People come from all over the world to visit and Doorkins sees them all. Everyone wants a selfie with her.

There's a whole team of people behind the scenes, running the cathedral and looking after its visitors. Doorkins sits with them when they sit down for a cup of tea and a slice of cake. She helps herself to a spot of milk and listens to everyone's plans for the week ahead.

On **Monday**, the school children come to learn about the history of the cathedral and all the incredible people who have been there. They draw pictures of the colourful stained glass windows and Doorkins helps them explore the ancient building.

Nobody knows all the secret nooks and crannies better than Doorkins.

On Tuesday, the choir comes to rehearse and the cathedral comes alive with the sound of music. The organ plays triumphantly and the choir sings the most spectacular songs. Nobody is usually allowed to listen to them practise, but the choirmaster makes an exception for Doorkins.

Doorkins loves listening to the music, and she's learnt not to try to join in while the choir is singing...

On Wednesday, the Bishop pays a visit, wearing a splendid red and gold robe and a tall pointed hat. He talks with all the people in the cathedral and is having a good time until someone points out that he has a cat hair on his back.

"Doorkins!" he exclaims, waving his crook. "How many times have I told you not to sit in my special chair!" But Doorkins pays no attention as she stretches her legs and sharpens her claws.

On **Thursday**, everyone is making preparations for a special visitor. Doorkins, being a very helpful cat, helps the flower arrangers with their flowers.

On **Friday**, Doorkins is still tired from all her hard work the day before. She finds a cosy spot on a plump red cushion and settles in for a nap.

When she wakes up, she finds the Dean wearing his best robe with a special visitor – Her Majesty the Queen!

On Saturday, the bells ring to celebrate a grand wedding. Doorkins admires the men in their fine suits and the ladies in their colourful hats. Everyone looks so nice, most beautiful of all is the bride in her elegant white dress.

As the ceremony begins, everyone turns to watch the bride as she is escorted down the aisle by her father... and Doorkins!

But **Sunday** is always Doorkins' favourite day of the week. It's when the cathedral is full of people from all around, joining together to sing songs, say prayers and worship God. Doorkins loves sitting right at the front of the congregation. After such a busy week, it's the time when Doorkins feels happiest and most content – and not just because there's always someone who'll scratch behind her ears.

At the end of the day, the candles are blown out, the floor is swept and the hymn books are neatly stacked away. It is time to close the cathedral doors for the night.

After Doorkins has had her supper, she's supposed to go out on mouse-catching duty. She would much rather play hide-and-seek with the Cathedral Vergers, though. Doorkins creeps down the stairs into the crypt...

...and there she settles down in a cosy spot and drifts off to sleep. Tomorrow will bring many new friends and more exciting adventures for Doorkins the Cathedral Cat.

But for now...she sleeps.

DOORKINS: THE REAL STORY

It **was on** one cold December morning in 2008 that a feral cat was found sitting on the doorstep of Southwark Cathedral, waiting for one of the Vergers to let her into the warm. At first she was an occasional visitor, alternating between the comfort of the cathedral and the leftover scraps from Borough Market. It didn't take long, however, for her to make the cathedral her permanent residence and she could be found waiting by the door each and every morning. Her spot by the entrance was what earned her the name "Doorkins".

Travellers, traders, "princes and paupers, prelates and prostitutes, poets, playwrights, prisoners and patients have all found refuge" at the church that has stood on this site since around 606 AD.* This culture of openness and inclusivity to all people (and cats) is at the very heart of Southwark Cathedral and its community.

---

*http://cathedral.southwark.anglican.org/community

The stories in this book are all based on true events from Doorkins' life. Visitors often find her napping in one of her many spots around the cathedral. Being a cat with both a well-developed sense of her own importance and little regard for formality, Doorkins has no compunctions about sleeping on the grandest chairs, and it was on one of these that HRH Queen Elizabeth found Doorkins when Her Majesty visited on the occasion of her Diamond Jubilee.

Doorkins has integrated herself into every aspect of cathedral life. While the Vergers are responsible for feeding her, all the other staff and volunteers know that Doorkins will inevitably stick her nose into their business, and so accept her as part of the team. Like any devout member of the cathedral community, Doorkins regularly attends services and congregants are often surprised - and pleased - by the sight of our feline attendant.

Doorkins' story is not unlike many of those at Southwark Cathedral, in that she came through the doors one day and never left. Like many of us, she felt at home here - safe, loved and accepted for who she was (even if we did think "she" was a "he" for her first few years). Like most of us, she's had a few bumps in the road, but despite all her foibles - or perhaps because of them - she has become a cherished member of the cathedral community.

PHOTOS

Picture 1   Doorkins outside Southwark Cathedral. Photograph reproduced by permission of the Leprosy Mission.

Picture 2   Doorkins at the door, waiting to be let in. Photograph copyright of Southwark Cathedral.

Picture 3   Doorkins eating her breakfast. Photograph copyright of Southwark Cathedral.

Picture 4   Doorkins flower arranging. Photograph copyright of Southwark Cathedral.

Picture 5   Doorkins in the Southwark Cathedral churchyard. Photograph reproduced by permission of The Gentle Author, Spitalfieldslife.com.

Picture 6   Doorkins sunbathing in the churchyard. Photograph copyright of Southwark Cathedral.

Picture 7   Doorkins sunning herself by the pulpit. Photograph copyright of Southwark Cathedral.

Picture 8   Doorkins sitting on a stack of kneelers. Photograph reproduced by permission of Tamsin Schwab.

Picture 9   Doorkins sleeping on the Bishop of Croydon's throne. Photograph copyright of Southwark Cathedral.

Picture 10   Doorkins organising the service sheets. Photograph reproduced by permission of Michael Lawson.

Picture 11   Doorkins keeps a close eye on the choristers! Photograph reproduced by permission of Tamsin Schwab; painting by Celia Pike.

Picture 12   Jamie the Verger prepares Doorkins' supper. Photograph reproduced by permission of Simon Gutwein and Jamie Collins.

Picture 13   Doorkins attends a busy service. Photograph reproduced by permission of Diocese of Southwark Communications.

Picture 14   Her Majesty Queen Elizabeth II and the Very Reverend Andrew Nunn, Dean of Southwark Cathedral, discover a sleeping Doorkins. Photograph copyright of the Press Association.

Picture 15   Her Majesty Queen Elizabeth II finds out more about Doorkins. Photograph reproduced by permission of Diocese of Southwark Communications.

Picture 16   The Cathedral Vergers ensure Doorkins' nap times are not disturbed. Photograph reproduced by permission of The Gentle Author, Spitalfieldslife.com.

Picture 17   The Cathedral Vergers, custodians of Doorkins, having tea. Photograph reproduced by permission of The Very Reverend Andrew Nunn, Dean of Southwark Cathedral.

Picture 18   Doorkins finds a quiet spot to sleep through morning Mass. Photograph reproduced by permission of Simon Gutwein.

Lisa Gutwein works as a medical doctor. She lives in London with her husband Simon, who is a Verger at Southwark Cathedral, and her two cats Matilda and Noah. Like Doorkins, Lisa wandered into Southwark Cathedral one day and never left!

Rowan Ambrose works in a general dental practice. She lives in London with her fiancé James and their dog Kizzie, who is now hoping to have her own series of illustrated books.
Rowan has always loved drawing, and is in her element with a pencil and a sketchpad to hand.

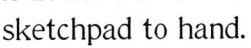